Canna'

Recipes for recr

by E...

This book has been written and self
published by Eric

Printed in the United Kingdom
1st Printing Year 2000
The First Edition
Photographs by Mayhem
Illustrations by Sunshine

1

Cannabis
for lunch

Peaceful Days
in crazy times

In sickness and in health

Someone once said
If I ate a lot of pot
I would never get out of bed!
I would sit all day
And put everything off until tomorrow instead.

They said, if I ate pot,
I would lose my head, and my job.
I would become addicted and waffle a lot.
It's true that's what they said.

Not only that but my eyes would turn red,
And my stomach all green,
I would end up with an attitude problem,
And become real mean.

So I just couldn't wait,
And started baking loads of hash cake.
It brought peace to my head,
Relieved the pains in my leg,
Put a smile on my face,
And brought laughter into everything I said.

Just shows, you can't believe all that is said.
And once through the propaganda and lies
It is now time for me to tell them
To put more pot and less pork in their pies!

Thank you

To all family and friends, without whom I would still be on
page one.
Also special thanks to all the campaign groups and individuals
who have shared their knowledge making this book possible.
Liz for putting all the pots and dots into their right places.
Trucky for typesetting, cover design and layout.
And most of all to all our fans who bought our first book
Cooking with Ganja.
Nice one!

Contents

Oven Temperatures

	C	F	Gas
Very cool	110	225	¼
	120	250	½
Cool	140	275	1
	150	300	2
Moderate	160	325	3
	180	350	4
Moderately hot	190	375	5
	200	400	6
Hot	220	425	7
	230	450	8
Very hot	240	475	9

Approximate Weights and Measures

Ounces	Grams
$\frac{1}{32}$	.75
$\frac{1}{16}$	1.75
$\frac{1}{8}$	3.5
$\frac{1}{4}$	7
$\frac{1}{2}$	14
1oz	28
2oz	57
3oz	85
4oz (1/4 lb)	113
5oz	142
6oz	170
7oz	198
8oz (1/2 lb)	227
16oz (1 lb)	454

Pint	Millilitre	U.S. oz
¼	142	$\frac{2}{3}$ CUP
½	283	1¼ CUPs
¾	425	2 CUPs
1 PINT	567	2½ CUPs
1½	851	3¾ CUPs
2	992	5 CUPs

U.S. Measures

1lb Butter	=	2 cups
1lb Flour	=	4 cups
1lb Sugar	=	2 cups
1lb Icing Sugar	=	3 cups
8oz Rice	=	1 cup

Rough Guide to Usage

WEIGHT	TYPE	PEOPLE/EFFECT	
1/6TH OUNCE (1.75 GRAMS)	CANNABIS RESIN	12	MELLOW
		8	STONED
		4	SMASHED
1/8TH OUNCE (3.5 GRAMS)	CANNABIS RESIN	20	MELLOW
		15	STONED
		8	SMASHED
1/8TH OUNCE (3.5 GRAMS)	BUDS	15	MELLOW
		10	STONED
		5	SMASHED
1 OUNCE (56 GRAMS)	LEAVES	15	MELLOW
		10	STONED
		5	SMASHED

Mellow is for therapeutic use
Stoned is for relaxing and enjoying
Smashed is for getting totally legless

Welcome

Welcome to the enchanting world of cannabis cookery.

The following pages will provide you with an informed and experienced guide into cooking with grass and resin in all its forms, from seeds to giant shade leaves.

We reveal the most effective ways to benefit both your mind and body, sharing with you the enjoyment of growing these beautiful plants, to preparing them in the kitchen. Creating some wonderful food that can be safely enjoyed. Bringing together the benefits for both recreational and therapeutic users.

It is a privilege for me to share the knowledge I have been entrusted with, some of which has remained secretly but securely handed down through generation to generation by people who have created medicinal preparations and pleasurable delights for many households.

Inspired by your warm response to "Cooking with Ganja" and the demand for me to look into more therapeutic cooking, I hope to delight you with this whole new range of delicious food and drinks recipes to suit your needs and to diminish any worries you may have regarding the use of cannabis.

Healing with Cannabis

Cannabis has been used to heal a great variety of conditions, and can be found regularly documented throughout our history. For those of us who are currently suffering and who would benefit from the relaxing and pain-relieving effects that cannabis can have, there is very little help on offer.

Their cry is loud, and I hope, not unheard for much longer.

At the back of this book you will find I have listed some good books available, which cover a lot of fascinating anecdotal evidence.

As more research is being carried out here in this country, we hope to see a great deal more evidence being recorded and published. For any of you who "surf the net", you will find an immense amount of information on cannabis. Its medicinal history stretches further than its recreational one. Throughout England, we have farmed the hemp plant for over eight hundred years, the word hemp originates from the old English word "hanf". Locally here in Dorset, the fields once stood proud with hemp and created a thriving industry based on its fine rope and nets. Now alas, it is relegated to museums and lost within folklore and stories, whilst her fields lay empty.

Cannabis has proven itself to be non-addictive and without any long-term side effects. Thankfully no-one can own the copyright or even begin to produce anything as good. It was not that long ago that cannabis was available on prescription in this country, until it was abolished in 1971. Its analgesic, antibiotic and anti-inflammatory properties were most effective when used as natural remedies. By eating cannabis you can enjoy the effects without having to take up smoking.

In the USA they have manufactured Marinol as a substitute for cannabis, but the results do not quite match up to those of the natural plant. It seems such a pointless exercise when rats supplied with extreme doses of THC are still healthier than they were ever expected to be.

Although like all things in life, it may not agree with you. Therefore, it is advisable to say that if you haven't tried any before, to just have a little at first attempt. If you are taking other prescribed drugs it is best to let your doctor know of your intentions.

...Healing with Cannabis

In this part of the book I would like to give you a brief summery of the recorded health problems that Cannabis is known to be of benefit to. I am not a medically trained person and therefore can only support these findings with the confidences of family and friends and the people who have written to me about their own personal experiences.

Cancer

For the patients themselves and the people who look after them, it is well known that cannabis can relieve some of the anxiety which occurs before treatment, and help with the recovery after chemotherapy.

This treatment can cause loss of appetite and dreadful nausea, which puts further strain on the body.

In this situation some people find they are only able to smoke a little cannabis until they are up to eating again. The effects from smoking act a lot quicker although they do not last for as long a time as when cannabis is eaten. Eating a very small amount can give noticeable relief for anything up to ten hours.

Epilepsy

In the case of epilepsy there has been a long history of cannabis being very effective in reducing seizures. In some instances, when taken regularly, either by eating small amounts or by smoking cannabis, the seizures have stopped..

Multiple Sclerosis

The benefits for people suffering with this illness have now been well publicised. Here in England, thanks to people like Clare Hodges and all the campaigners whose strength and conviction has shown that cannabis can help. For many of these people it can mean that some of the lost bodily functions caused by Multiple Sclerosis can be temporarily regained, bestowing a far better quality of day to day life.

Spasms

Spasms and jerks can be considerably reduced by the use of cannabis, as it helps to relax muscles. Smoking will bring the effects on within minutes, whereas food takes a good half an hour. This depends on whether you have eaten beforehand, as this will slow down the effect.

...Healing with Cannabis

AIDS

When Aids is crippling the body, many have found cannabis can help by reducing nausea and diarrhoea and in stimulating the appetite, offering the person gentle relief from some of the great strain and worry associated with this disease.

In such a vulnerable state it is important to be aware that there is a risk involved, and that some of the uncontrolled supplies may have been contaminated by the use of pesticides or other unknown substances. In order to avoid these pitfalls, either get to know your supplier or start your own garden.

Menstrual Cramps

I can tell you first hand, of the benefits for this complaint and believe me it did not take long to find many others who agreed with me! We have come to the conclusion that many women experience pain relief and far less build up of flatulence. We all agreed we were far less moody of course our menfolk agreed also!

I do hope this use will be recognised again, and we will all be able to eat pot once a month without breaking the law. It was quite acceptable in the days of Queen Victoria, who has been well noted for having Cannabis prescribed regularly from her physicians.

Glaucoma

This condition is a major cause of blindness, and there has been a great deal of research on this subject in the USA, the results of which have proven that cannabis can slow the rate of blindness considerably, and in some cases help to regain sight that has been lost.

Arthritis and Rheumatism

Pain relief can make such a tremendous difference to someone whose life is constantly ruled by pain. It can effect every part of your day and night and losing the pleasure of a good night's sleep can just add to the problems.

A small biscuit or cake eaten before bed, eases the pain away and can allow you to sleep a lot better, so that you wake up feeling refreshed and rested. These effects can go on lasting for up to two days, using a very small amount of cannabis.

...Healing with Cannabis

Insomnia

People who get stoned recreationally always finish up asleep, usually on your couch! You cannot overdose as you will feel light headed and wobbly on your feet and you will probably be sick. All you will want to do is lie down and sleep it off. This is the best way to cope with any of the effects you do not feel comfortable with.

By using small amounts, the effects are mild and a gentle relaxation is felt throughout the mind and body, often resulting in a restful sleep.

Asthma

Taking cannabis can relieve the symptoms of asthma but it needs to be inhaled to do this. The downside is that the hot smoke can trigger off an attack.

At present, the best way is using a vapourisation pipe. It is the cleanest and gentlest way to smoke, as it warms the cannabis, releasing the vapours instead of the fierce burning of a pipe.

Stress and Mild Depression

We all have to cope with life's stresses and sometimes this can become too much for us to cope with. Cannabis is used by millions of people to help relax and alleviate stress. It can also be a positive step away from the powerful drugs which are prescribed for this ailment. In the same way it is also commonly used by those who have relied too heavily on alcohol and other drug abuses, it can offer a helping hand on the road to recovery. However it is by no means a cure for all our problems, but it can help to stimulate a positive outlook and is not physically addictive. It is wise to be aware of the paranoia experienced by some people, and if you are not comfortable, you should not continue to use it.

Migraine

Some people have discovered that cannabis taken at the onset of an attack can help to reduce the pain and visual disturbances. Regular users have found that the attacks have stopped altogether, or as I personally have experienced they have become milder and less frequent.

...Healing with Cannabis

Labour and Childbirth

There is no proof of harm to the unborn baby according to some reports and others show a concerned argument for more research to be carried out.

Ultimately, it is a matter of personal choice, one of which most of us must make on our own as cannabis is not considered to be an option for Western women. No drugs of any kind has to remain the best option, but saying that, I used cannabis to control morning sickness during pregnancy. And I chose to eat a piece of hash cake when I went into labour and it kept me relaxed and in good humour, with little pain, for over eleven hours until my son arrived, rosy- cheeked and healthy.

Back Pain

This is a common complaint that cannabis can help to alleviate, whether suffering from severe spinal damage or general strain, the pain can be considerably eased.

"Hemp seed I set, hemp seed I sow,
The man that is my true love
Come after me and mow"

From old Dorset folklore comes this charming rhyme to be sung in the garden on midsummer whilst carrying a rake, and throwing seed over your right shoulder...and there standing behind you, will be your future husband scythe in hand!

HISTORY AT THE TABLE

Although not always approved of at the table, over the years the pleasures of eating cannabis and hemp have certainly endured. Recently I came across some wonderful references in a 18th Century book called: A Treatise on Hemp. (Marcandier, 1764). The French origin of this literature gives us an insight as to the uses of cannabis across Europe at that time. Much of it is still just as relevant today. Hemp was widely grown for the manufacture of rope, paper and hardwearing cloth known as canvas, a word that derives from cannabis. Its medicinal properties and humours effects were well known and an every day part of people's lives, but not with out some words of caution. I quote:

"Hemp seed is of a drying nature, that it weakens the generative powers in men, when eaten to excess!"

"Taken inwardly, or outwardly applied, it has not the dangerous qualities that are ascribed to the whole plant with its leaves; the powder of it, mixed with drink, will make those who use it drunk, dull, and stupid."

The book also mentions the "pleasure of fried desserts and little sweet cakes made with the plants leaves, to be eaten at collations and to promote drinking". Sounds good to me!

For daily ailments it suggests "pounding the leaves when they are still fresh in a mortar with butter and place on burns", Ouch!

And that "if the green juice is squeezed from the leaves it will attract insects and bring out all vermin that enter the ear, and infest it". Gladly we seem to have eradicated this complaint!

The Hemp oil is recommended as a laxative, helping to expel wind, and was sometimes eaten in soup. As today, its relaxing and pain reliving properties were recognised for inflammation and swelling of the joints.

Of course the history of this plant goes back a lot further to its countries of origin. In India, Africa and China the cannabis plant has long sustained people and animals with an essential food source of proteins and nutrients, and it is also regarded for its use in veterinary practice. It has also played an important part in religious and spiritual gatherings around the world.

In India there are records dating from 800 B.C. One of the oldest recorded recipes is for Bhang. It was considered to be a general household remedy, the boiled leaves in milk were given for a persistent cough and it is still used in this way today.

...History at the table

It is in India that we discover the first mention of the recreational and spiritual use of cannabis. Previous records date from as far back as the 27th century B.C in China, where the plant was mainly used for medicinal purposes. Many of the recipes were spoken or worded in rhyme. At the present time, recipes for the use of cannabis are still not in great abundance. There are however some wonderful references to be found. "The Modern herbal" 1931, written by mrs M Grieve, informs us as to the different names given to the Indian Bahng paste made with milk and of pastes and emulsions made with fats. These are now referred to as cannabutter or the sacred Ghee of India. In Tibet they are called Momea or Mimea, and in Cairo it is referred to as Mapouchari and Arabians call it Dawames. She also refers to a mixture of honey and hashish powder known as Madjound in Algeria and of little round flat cakes called hashish made in Russia, which are also found in central Asia where they are called Nasha.

"Stick a few fresh green branches collected in the spring and place in you bed. This will keep all the bed bugs away".

"It is regarded as dangerous to sleep in a field of hemp, owing to the aroma".

As anyone who has slept next to a few plants in the bedroom will be more than aware of.

For Gonorrhoea

"Take equal parts of tops from the female and male plants. Bruise in a mortar to express the juice and mix in an equal amount of alcohol. Take 1-3 drops every two - three hours"

I should think this could cure almost anything!

Alice B. Toklas (USA) had her first cannabis brownie recipe censored in the 1954 edition of her cook book. However, in later editions, she shared with us the delights of "Hashish Majoon", a Moroccan recipe made with fruit, nuts and spices, all combined with butter and cannabis. This, no doubt, was the inspiration for a lot of the American books which followed, notably "The Art and Science of Cooking With Cannabis" (1973) which refers to Majoon as the name for hashish jam made in some parts of India.

Retsina is the name given to a potent wine made with hashish by the Greeks. "Cooking With Ganja" which I first published in England 1994 has helped revive this art, once again bringing together old traditions and welcoming new ones.

BASIC PREPARATIONS

<u>BUDS:</u> Try not to handle too much, hold by the stalk and snip finely with a good pair of scissors over a clean bowl, so you're sure to catch all those wonderful crystals.

<u>LEAVES</u>: Rinse the leaves and bring to the boil in water, strain and grind with a little milk to make Bhang paste, the water will not absorb the essential properties.

You can also hang them in a warm place to dry, then remove stalks and grind leaves to a fine powder, this is called Hemp or leaf flour.

<u>SEEDS</u>: Nutty in flavour, soaked in water and ground to a pulp which can be added to other foods or made into a natural health drink.

<u>RESIN</u>: Warmed gently in a small metal bowl and crumbled to a fine powder, it gives the appearance of other common ground spices, now ready for cooking.

<u>OIL</u>: Use in very small amounts and respect its strength! It is regarded as a class (A) drug and often carries heavier penalties.

<u>HEMP OIL</u>: Only contains trace THC, made from the seeds it is a healthy alternative, although because of its richness it should be used sparingly.

As a Guide

If smoking for therapeutic use start with a very small piece of hash the size of a small pea, about a quarter gram, to start with this should be sufficient, also for in drinks for one person. If you are using buds use half a teaspoon to measure for one. If it is leaves that you have, they can often be a little harsh to smoke and cooking them is a much more enjoyable way of getting the best out of them. Because the THC content is less, you often need quite a bit more which does make them unsuitable for some recipes.

The guides are broken-down to suit both recreational and therapeutic users, as in some cases we have found there can be a considerable difference in the amounts generally being used. The measurements are based on good average stock, not super strength, and that you wish to be pleasantly stoned. Sometimes your cannabis may be weaker – therefore you will need to add a little more than suggested. You will soon know what suits you as you begin to experiment with different types. Once you have prepared your cannabis in any form do not leave it exposed for long periods, as it will begin to lose some of its potency.

From the garden

Hashish, Resin, Pot and Charis all refer to the solid forms of cannabis made from the plants most potent flowering tops. Those grown in the hottest climates or in controlled conditions, grow to great strength with a high THC content. Sadly the quality of imported resin has deteriorated considerably over the last twenty years or so, such is the demand the world over.

Hash comes in many different textures and colours varying from a light caramel brown through to deep dark olive to black, sometimes with a tint of the darkest green. The texture varies from soft and oily to light and crumbly, or rock hard. To test, warm slightly and smell, if it bubbles or smells unnatural don't use it. It should have an earthy or a pungent sweetness about it.

Ganja, grass and leaves refer to the plant in its raw form before preparation, often hung to dry and used as it is. The large shade leaves are less potent but still effective. Plants come in many varieties and strengths, the weakest with only trace THC is hemp. With good seed supply, home-grown Ganja can be very successful.

To the Kitchen!

Utensils you will need:

Pestle and mortar, or a bowl and milk bottle, some weighing scales and a fine sieve or muslin cloth, scissors, poaching spoon, chopping board, greaseproof paper, and finally...a small metal bowl to save your fingers when heating the hash! A food processor is handy to chop up leaves, some basic kitchen equipment, and a little of your time!

Always prepare you cannabis first
And save the washing up 'till last
Never let it boil or burn, or try to cook it fast

Wash you hands before you start
And grind the weed with all your heart
This really is the hardest part.

Keep tiny fingers out of the way
Or children could end up stoned all day
What would the teacher say?

Do not give without telling all
As nobody likes to be made the fool
Share with your friends, and stay cool.

Seed Stuff

Seeds, thankfully, are becoming more available as a health food for us and not just for the budgies. They only contain traces of THC (Delta 9 –tetrahydrocannabinol) the naughtiest of the 60 cannabinoids that have been found in Cannabis, so their trade in England is still permitted as we go to print. High in nutritional value they are very versatile for cooking and in cosmetics. Used as a skin softener the paste is gentle and soothing. It is also said eating them could help to lower blood pressure. Ground into fine flour (gluten free) you can use it as an alternative to wheat flour.

They can be gently toasted and sprinkled onto desserts such as pancakes.or added to a wide variety of savoury dishes. Once sprouted, they are a nice addition to salads.

They are also pressed and made into oil and butters. The seeds are specially organically grown for eating and should be bought from a quality stockist, you'll find some helpful addresses at the back.

Seed Preparation

Originating from Ancient China, the following preparation is a sacred and inspiring recipe, which comes from the kind hands of Hempseed Organics.

Hemp Star Milk (Houma)

A drop of love, clean hands
4oz /125g Organic Hempseed
1 pint of distilled or filtered water (warm)
7 Almonds
Fruit or vegetable juice of your choice

Method

Clean through the seed throwing out any small/green
immature or damaged ones. Place into a bowl and cover with
water. Stir gently and scoop out all the healthy floating seeds,
place into a clean bowl with almonds and soak for eight hours
then change the water and continue to soak for 36 hours,
changing the water regularly to stop any fermentation.

The seeds will start to split and poke out their tails after
soaking. They are now ready to drain and grind in your pestle
and mortar, adding a drop of water and love as its hard work by
hand. Using a grinder is easier. Place into a jug and add warm
distilled water and stir gently leaving to rest for 10 minutes.
Prepare your fruit or vegetable juices, then strain the milk
gently into a clean jug, ready to drink. As it is or add your
chosen juice, banana and mango are especially good. The milk
sadly has no shelf life and must be drunk straight away.

Seed Salubrious

Hemp seed has 500 calories per 100 grams.

Soluble fibre makes up 3% of the seed, containing approx. 32% insoluble C60 organic carbon fibre, and 20-25 % protein. Approx. 30% of the seed is unsaturated fat and is the lowest in saturated fats at 8% of total oil volume. This gives us the highest total percentage of Essential Fatty Acids known alongside other common plants.

The seeds also contain a whole range of important minerals and vitamins A, B1, B2, B6, B3, C, D, E.

You should always wash seeds thoroughly before grinding them or soaking in water until they start to sprout. This softens the shell, ready to add to your recipe. They can be lightly toasted on a baking tray, when the first one pops remove from the heat, ready to add to soups, salads, curries, pasta, and a favourite of ours flap jacks. Seeds are delicate and will turn rancid soon after being exposed to cooking . It is advised you eat them within 24 hours of preparation.

The oil from seeds has a nutty richness which makes it like the raw seed, unsuitable for frying. It should be used as a table oil, kept in the fridge or freezer away from light in a well sealed bottle, or it will also turn rancid. If it is required on a daily basis 1-tablespoon is adequate.

ANCIENT PREPARATIONS

Cannabis can be added to the hemp star milk when it is finally resting in warm water for the last 10 minutes. The natural fat of the seeds will absorb the THC recreating this ancient method of preparing a potent drink or cooking juice without the use of any animal fats, sugars or alcohol.

Bhang paste

Made easily by using ground seeds and adding ground grass and a little milk to make this excellent cooking paste. Or simply grind your grass with a little milk

If you are using hemp oil, a tablespoon full, warmed for 5 minutes with powdered cannabis added makes a potent mix ready for cooking. If cannabis is boiled or over cooked it will destroy the THC. With gentle cooking the fats will absorb it all and can only improve the strength and flavour increasing the potency by up to 4 times.

You can also add lecithin found naturally in both cow and soya milk. This can be bought in powdered form from health food shops, and works as an emulsifier helping to evenly absorb and distribute the fats which absorb the THC. Add about 3 - 4 teaspoons to your recipe and it will improve potency. It is very useful in soups and dressings where the oil tends to separate.

Indian Bhang

1/8th oz (3.5g) butter
2 cups of milk
1-2 grams of hash or grass
A pinch of spice

Method

Melt the butter in a pan add cannabis simmer for one minute, then add milk and warm gently. Add spices, cinnamon and nutmeg are good you may also like to add some honey to taste.

If you want to give it a kick add some vodka!

We also found that instead of milk you can use apple juice or better still, cider.

Hasty Pudding

Or porridge as it is now known.

This ancient gruel originates from China and can either be eaten as porridge or added to soup.

Ingredients (for two)
1 cup (113g) 4oz hemp seed
2 cups of water
1-2 grams of hash or grass
Milk
Honey

Method

First Soak and grind or toast and grind the seeds until they are really fine, then put into a pan with the water and bring to the boil. Simmer on low heat. Add Ganja if desired and cook for 10 minutes. Add honey and milk, or add to soup as you would a stock.

Hemp Oil and Maple Dressing

3 tablespoons balsamic vinegar
6 tablespoons hemp oil
1 teaspoon cumin powder
3 tablespoons maple syrup
Method

If you wish, add three teaspoons of ground grass or one teaspoon of crumbled hash.

Put all ingredients into a screw-top jar and shake well. Keep in the fridge, you can use different oils and other herbs such as Olive and Tarragon.

Sacred Ghee

Originating from India this is a useful butter that can be added to many dishes and it will keep for over a month without refrigeration.

1/2 lb. (225g) butter
1/2 oz (14g) of good buds. Or 1-oz (28g) leaves.
For a mellower effect use
1/4oz(7g) buds or 1/2 oz leaves

Heat the butter slowly and as it comes to the boil remove the froth off the top and discard it, continue until the frothing has stopped.

Lower the heat and add the finely ground grass, stirring gently (hash dissolves quicker). Keep on the lowest heat for approximately 15 minutes then strain collecting all the butter into a jar.

If you want to make a simple version known as CANNABUTTER then just melt your butter and add the cannabis without preparing the ghee. If using hash resin there is no need to strain. This is fine if you are going to use it within 2 weeks. Where a recipe calls for butter you can substitute some or all with sacred ghee or cannabutter.

The Old Wives Brew

Cannabis is often added to alcohol to make a quick and effective drink. In "Cooking with Ganja" you will find the cooks booze and fruity wine which are both easy to do and keep for years. This red-hot little number is however best drank on the night of making, and merry making will definitely follow!

1 bottle of red wine
4 cloves
¼ teaspoon of nutmeg
¼ teaspoon of cardamom
A stick (or ground) cinnamon
An orange to stick the cloves into
⅛ or ¼ oz Prepared buds or crumbled hash
For leaves use around ½ oz

Method

Place all ingredients into a pan and warm gently for 2 hours. This is enough for 6-8 people

SOMETHING FOR LUNCH

Savoury Flapjacks

4oz (113g) butter or marge'
4oz (113g) rolled oats
4oz (113g) hemp seeds (soaked)
4oz (113g) grated cheese
A small amount of grated onion if desired
½ teaspoon mustard powder
Salt/pepper
1 egg
⅛th oz hash/ground buds
For a mellower effect use 1/6th
Or use between ¼ - ⅛th of ground leaves

Method

Heat your oven to 400f /200c

Cream your butter and add everything. Mix well, press into a greased tin and cook for 30 minutes. Cool and cut into squares. Makes about 10.

Hemp Union Pasta

½ lb (225g) hemp seed flour
Or you can use grass leaf flour
½ lb (225g) plain flour or Italian pasta flour
A pinch of salt
4 eggs
1 tablespoon of cold pressed hemp oil

Method

Mix the flours and salt onto a wooden board. Make a well in the centre and drop in the eggs and oil. Using your hands, mix oil and eggs together and gradually draw in the flour to form a stiff dough. Knead for about 15 minutes until smooth and elastic. Wrap in polythene and leave to relax in a cool place for one hour.

Roll one small piece of dough at a time until paper thin. Cut into required shapes.

Allow to dry; hang long noodles over a clean broom handle suspended between two chairs; lay small shapes on a wire rack for 30 minutes before boiling.

AFTERNOON TEA

Fairy Bread

The Fairy bread is sweet and kind
But eat too much and you'll blow your mind!

1 cup of black tea
3 eggs
6oz(170g) butter
8oz(227g) brown sugar
12oz(340g) mixed dried fruit
12oz(340g) self raising wheatmeal flour
1 teaspoon mixed spice and cinnamon

⅛th oz ground buds or hash
Or ¼ oz leaves
For a mellow effect use ¹⁄₁₆th oz buds/hash
or ⅛th oz leaves

Method

Set oven to 325f 160c, put the tea, butter, sugar, fruit and
cannabis into a pan and simmer very gently for 15 minutes.
Remove from the heat and beat in the flour, spices and eggs.
Put into a greased 8 inch tin and bake for 2 hours. To test,
prod with a skewer into the centre. If the skewer comes out
clean the cake is ready. Cool and slice into approximately eight
and spread with butter.

Gingerbread

(Suitable for non-sugar diets)

8oz (225g) of pear or apple spread
½ pint (300ml) milk
4oz (113g) marge'/butter
12oz (350g) wholemeal flour/hemp flour
2oz (50g) sultanas
4 tsp ground ginger
2 tsp lemon juice
2 tsp bicarbonate of soda
2 tbsp boiling water
⅛th oz of Prepared cannabis, hash or buds
Or for a mellow effect use ⅛th oz of hash or buds

Method

Heat oven to 180c /350f and grease an 8 inch cake tin. Place spread, milk, lemon juice, marge', cannabis and ginger into a pan. Heat gently until melted.

Mix the flour and sultanas in one bowl, then mix bicarbonate and boiling water together. Add to the flour mix along with your cannabis mixture and give it a good beating! Pop into the tin and bake for 35 minutes until firm and risen, cool and cut into 16, allowing 1-2 each.

A Little Sponge Cake

Paper cases
6oz (170g) plain flour
6oz (170g) margarine
6oz (170g) sugar
3 eggs
3 tsp. baking powder
A drop of milk
Prepare ⅛th oz of hash or buds to a fine powder.
For a mellow effect use ⅛th oz

Easy method

Heat the oven to 180c/350f

Beat the lot together until thick and smooth then spoon into around 30 paper cases.

Or a little fake cake

Buy a packet-mix and make up as instructed. If you wish to control the amount of cannabis going into each cake, just add a little to each case. Before baking stir it in with a handle of a teaspoon.

Bake for 25 to 30 minutes, until golden and bouncy to the touch. They can then be frozen and defrosted when needed.

SWEET SHOP DREAMS

Into the sweetie shop we go
When we will be out nobody knows
It's full of chewy, sticky things
Made from little children's' dreams

Chocolate drunken truffles cover the floor
Soft caramel's drip long from the door
The chairs are made of marshmallows and fudge
This place is full with chocolate and love

Jars of candy and Turkish Seeds
Although not all is quite as it seems
Its those little hash nuts you see
I ate a few too many.

Drunken Truffles

Taking the struggle out of the truffle.

This is the easiest way I found yet to make a good truffle. They will keep for weeks in an airtight container in the fridge.

8oz (225g) plain chocolate
1 tbs. (15ml) condensed milk
1 cap of spirit, or liquor, ginger wine is good.
⅛th hash or buds
Or use ½oz ground leaves
For a mellow effect use ⅛th oz
Or use ¼oz ground leaves

Method

Melt chocolate in a bowl over hot water (not boiling)

Then add milk, cannabis and booze. Remove from the heat, beat well and leave to cool then dust your fingers in coco powder and roll into truffle balls. Makes around 20 in less than 10 minutes.

Loaded toffee caramel's

These are excellent to disguise in toffee wrappers and take with you and share as we did in Hyde Park, London '97 '98 May Day '99.

3oz (85g) butter
¼ can condensed milk
8oz (227g) sugar
8 tbs. golden syrup
½ tsp. vanilla essence
4oz (113g) plain chocolate (broken up)
⅛th *hash finely crumbled*
For a mellower effect use ⅛th
(Grass does not work as well as hash in this one)
You will need a heavy-based pan as this gets extremely hot

Method

Put everything except chocolate and hash into the heavy-based saucepan. Stir over a low heat until the sugar has dissolved.

Add the broken chocolate and boil steadily to 120 degrees centigrade. If you don't have a thermometer, put a drop of cold water into a saucer and drop a little of the toffee onto it. As it cools it will show the stage that it has reached. For a soft caramel, roll into a soft ball. The hotter it becomes the more toffee like and harder it will set.

Remove the pan from the heat and place on a cold surface. When it has settled and cooled to 60c, the hash can be gently and safely stirred into the mixture.

Pour into a buttered 8-inch tin after it has cooled down enough to handle. Cut into about 30 squares or roll into eclairs. If you wish to add a touch of luxury, dip into melted chocolate. These will keep for several weeks wrapped in waxed paper and placed in a tin.

Mellow-out fudge

2oz (57g) butter
4oz (113g) plain chocolate (broken)
2 tbs. cream
4oz (113g) marsh mallows (white)
4oz (113g) icing sugar
½ teaspoon vanilla essence or booze
2oz (57g) chopped nuts (or crushed biscuits)
Prepared cannabis
⅛th oz hash or buds
For a mellower effect use 1/6th
Or a ¼oz of ground leaves

Method

Using a double pan or a bowl over a pan of simmering water, melt chocolate and then add butter and cream. Add the cannabis, booze or essence and marsh mallows stirring gently. When it has all melted, add the icing sugar. Stir until smooth and remove from the heat. Finally add the nuts.

Pours into an 8 inch buttered tin and allow to cool, then cut into squares. This is an easy fudge which also freezes well and tastes wicked!

Ganja candy

In 1860 the Ganjah Wallah Hashish Co, USA made and sold maple sugar candy with added hashish which was most popular.

Microwave

2oz (50g) butter
12oz (350g) soft brown sugar
¼ pint (150ml) milk
½ tsp. vanilla essence
Prepared cannabis
⅛th oz hash or buds
For a mellower effect use 1/6th
(Not to good with leaves)

Method

Place butter in a deep glass dish melt for 2 minutes. Add all ingredients apart from the hash. Cook uncovered for 3-4 minutes until it begins to boil. Remove from heat and stir well.

Return and cook for a further 4 minutes, remove and stir. Cook for a further 4 minutes. Once the mixture has settled, stir in your finely prepared cannabis and beat until it gleams. Pour into a 8 inch buttered tin. When set, break into pieces.

Turkish Seed Sweets

4oz (125g) hemp seeds
4oz (125g) flaked coconut
4oz (125g) flaked almonds
2oz (56g) sunflower seeds
1oz (28g) sesame seeds
150ml honey
2oz (56g) butter
⅛th oz powdered hash or buds
¼th oz for a mellower effect

Method

Gently simmer the cannabis and seeds (except the sesame seeds) in the butter. Stir over the heat for five minutes, do not let the mixture brown. Remove from the heat and stir in the honey, almonds and coconut and spread thinly over a plate. When cool enough roll into small balls and roll in sesame seeds. These only keep for a day in the fridge as they always get eaten.

Hash nuts

4 tbs. peanut butter
6 tbs. golden syrup or honey
4oz (113g) powdered milk
2oz (57g) desiccated coconut
4oz (113g) sesame seed
Prepared cannabis.
⅛th oz hash or buds
For a mellower effect use 1/6th
Or ¼oz ground leaves

Method

Butter an 8-inch tin. Put the syrup, cannabis and peanut butter into a pan, heat gently and stir until smooth. Add the powdered milk, coconut, and seeds, mix well and turn into your tin. Cool and cut into squares, making around 32 which will keep for up to three weeks in an airtight container in the fridge.

BACK AFTER LUNCH

> Hashish fills the chambers of my mind with
> understanding and love
> and my belly with excitement

Potted Pot

1 egg
3oz (85g) plain flour
6fl oz milk
Half a small onion finely chopped
2oz (57g) finely chopped ham
2oz (57g) cheese (something nice)
⅛th finely ground hash or buds
Or a ⅛th ground leaves

Method

Heat the oven to 200c /400f and grease a 12 holed bun tin.

Mix the egg, flour and milk until smooth, then stir in the
onion, ham, cheese, and cannabis. Pour into each hole to
about half full, and bake for 15-20 minutes. When they are
brown and risen, allow to cool before loosening from the tin.
Serves 1-2 each

Hash stuffed peaches

8 ripe peaches
10oz (284g) pork sausage meat cooked and drained
3 medium new potatoes cooked and grated
1 green pepper and one small onion finely chopped
1/2 tsp. Basil, 1/2 tsp. Sage
2oz (56g) butter
2tbs.of whisky
Prepared cannabis
⅛th oz hash or buds
For a mellower effect use 1/32nd
Or ⅛th oz leaves finely ground.

Method

Wash peaches and cut in half removing the stone. In the a large bowl mix everything except butter and whisky. Melt half the butter in a frying pan, add the meat mixture and press down firmly. Cook for around 5 minutes until crispy then remove onto a plate. Melt the remaining butter and cook the other side.

Spoon some into each peach, drizzle on some whisky and pop into a warmed oven for 10 minutes ready to serve, two each.

Crackers

Makes around 40
4oz (113g) cheese grated
3oz (85g) butter
4oz (113g) flour
2oz (57g) chopped nuts
1 tbs. Garlic paste
Little drop of milk
Salt/pepper
2oz (57g) hemp seeds washed ground
½oz or ¼oz leaves (finely ground)

Method

Mix the whole lot together except the hemp seed to make a dough and add a little milk, if the mixture is too dry. Then cut in half and roll into two sausage shapes about 6 inches long. Wrap in plastic bags and pop in the fridge until firm, about 2 hours.

Heat the oven to 200c /400f and cut each sausage into 1/4 inch (10cm) rounds and roll in ground seeds. Place on a baking sheet with a little space between each, bake for 5 - 8 minutes until golden. Store in an airtight tin.

Little Pea

10oz (284g) tinned chick peas
1 onion finely chopped
1 egg (beaten)
1 clove of garlic crushed
3tbs, hemp seed tahini
1tsp cumin powder
4oz (113g) breadcrumbs, and a little flour
½oz ground leaves or ⅛th crumbled hash
For a mellower effect use ¼oz leaves or ⅛th hash

Method

To make tahini

4oz (113g) hemp seeds roasted until they begin to pop ground as fine as you can. Add 1 tbs. of hemp or sesame seed oil and blend. If it is a little dry add a drop of water.

Heat the oven to 180c/350f and drain the peas then mash. Add everything else. Mix and divide into small balls. Dust-in flour and use to stiffen mixture if needed, then bake on a greased baking tray for 15-20 minutes, or fry until golden.

Honey and Oil

Cannabis plants grown in hot climates naturally produce oil. It is collected by rubbing your hands onto the plants and then scraping off all the oil collected. It can also be extracted from hashish and purified to different stages The oil is highly potent and should be treated with respect. If you do have some oil it is traditional to add it to honey. We have also found that this recipe works just as well with hashish or flowering buds.

Method

Heat 1tbs of butter or ghee for each gram of oil used. Or 1/8th very finely ground hash/buds to 1tbs butter.

Stir over a low heat with 1/2 a cup of runny honey until well combined and pour into jars. Allow to cool before putting the lids on.

One teaspoon is a good starting amount on your morning toast or added to hot water and tea or even used straight from the jar!

SWEET STICKY SOFT AND SAUCY
AND JUST A LITTLE NAUGHTY!

Hash oats

4oz(113g) marge'/butter
3oz(85g) porridge oats
4oz(113g) self raising flour or hemp leaf flour
4oz (113g) sugar
1oz (28g) coco
1 tbs. golden syrup
1oz(28g) chocolate drops/buttons
⅛th hash or buds
Or ¼oz ground leaves
For a mellower effect use
⅛th hash or buds or ⅛th leaves

Method

Heat the oven to 220c/425f

Melt the marge', sugar, coco, syrup and finely prepared cannabis in a large pan over a low heat. When it has all melted remove from the heat. Add the flour and oats, stir in well and pour into an 8 inch greased tin. Place on a high shelf in the oven for 10 minutes. Take out and sprinkle on the chocolate buttons and allow to cool in the tin before cutting into squares.

Mr. Nice Cake

10oz (285g) caster sugar
6oz(170g) marge'/butter
3 eggs
1tsp vanilla essence
6oz (170g) fromage frais
8oz (227g) s/r flour
2oz (57g) cocoa
2oz (57g) dark chocolate (grated)
1 tsp. bicarbonate of soda
⅛th oz buds or hash
Or ½oz ground leaves
For a mellower effect use ⅛th oz hash or ¼oz of leaves

Method

Heat the oven to170c 325f

Grease a 9 inch cake tin and dust in flour.

Beat the sugar, marge' and cannabis together then beat in the eggs, essence, and fromage frais. Stir in cocoa, chocolate, flour and bicarbonate of soda then mix until smooth. Pour into tin and bake for 40-45 minutes. Test with a skewer if it comes out clean the cake is ready. Cover in thick icing or cream. 8-10 servings.

Cannabis Cookies

(Suitable for sugar free diets)

Makes 24
7oz (200g) flour
2oz (57g) marge'
2oz (57g) peanut butter
4oz (115g) minced raisins
1egg
1tsp bicarbonate of soda
½ tsp. baking powder
1tsp vanilla essence
4 tbs. of milk
¼oz leaves or ⅛th oz bud finely prepared.
For a mellower effect use ⅛th oz leaves or ⅟₁₆th buds

Method

Heat the oven to 170c/325f and grease two baking sheets ready.

Mix the raisins, cannabis, peanut butter and marge'. Beat in the egg, essence and milk, and then gently add the flour, baking powder and bicarbonate of soda. Place on to trays in spoonfuls, brush with a little milk and cook for 15 minutes. Try and allow to cool before eating!

Glastonbury Mud Cake

6oz (170g) butter
2tbs hemp oil
8oz (227g) dark chocolate (grated)
4 eggs separated
8oz (227g) caster sugar
3oz (85g) s/r flour
Black hash is especially good use $\frac{1}{8}$th or $\frac{1}{16}$th oz
Or fresh oily buds finely chopped

Method

Heat the oven to 190c/375f and grease an 8-inch loose-based tin. Separate the eggs and beat the whites until stiff.

In another bowl beat together the egg yolks and the sugar then cream-in the butter Add chocolate, cannabis, hemp oil and flour. Then fold in the egg whites and pour into your tin. Bake on the middle shelf for 1½ hours. Mud has never been so good!

Jammin Banana Jam

6 bananas and 3 oranges and 2 lemons!
⅛ th or ¼oz hash finely crumbled
2 capsful of fruit wine or spirit of choice
1 –1 1/2 lb. (450g)– (675g) sugar

Method

Cut the bananas into small pieces, place oranges and lemons into a pan of warm water then squeeze the juice and mix into the banana pulp. Add 3/4lb–(340g) sugar to every 1lb (450g) of fruit. Boil slowly for 30 to 45 minutes then remove from the heat. Wait for it to settle then pour in wine. Stir in the hash, allow to cool and then pour into jars. This keeps well and is ideal on toast or to fill jam tarts.

Toffee Sauce

2oz (57g) butter
4oz (114g) brown sugar
5floz golden syrup or maple syrup
5floz double cream
Few drops of vanilla essence
⅛th finely powdered hash

Method

Put butter, sugar and syrup into a pan on a low heat. Once the sugar has dissolved, add essence, hash and cream. Stir gently for a few minutes then pour into a jug. This is delicious with ice cream or over puddings and cakes. If you want it thicker for making a toffee flan then add less cream.

TINCTURES AND OINTMENT

Tinctures are easily made using dried grass finely ground and covered in alcohol. One pint to every ounce of dried buds, or if you are using leaves use 2oz (56g) to every pint of alcohol. This is best done into a dark glass bottle with a screw lid, allow the tincture to rest for two weeks in a dark warm place. always make sure utensils are sterilised clean with boiling water.

Your alcohol needs to be at least thirty proof, 60% alcohol content or even higher. Vodka is the most readily available. Give the mixture a good shake once a day and then strain through a fine filter and store in a dark tinted glass bottle to preserve the tincture. This can now be added to drinks or food, try one drop at first as the potency can vary.

Blackcurrant blowout

1tbs blackcurrant juice in cup and boiling water to fill the cup. Add a few drops of tincture. Or crumble in 1g of hash and add a shot of vodka

Ointment

This is also easily made using Vaseline. Take 2oz (56g) and warm in a pan with 2 oz (957g) butter and 1oz (28g) finely ground leaves for 10 minutes. Pour back into the Vaseline jar and store in a dark place. This can now be rubbed on aching tired joints or on dry rough skin.

Poultices and body potions

The large shade leaves can be soaked in alcohol and then wrapped directly onto swollen joints, or they can be pulped and warmed with a little water and placed on affected area such as sores or ulcers, and sunburn. Hold in place with a wrap of wet cloth. If the skin is inflamed wrap the pulp in a thin cotton cloth so it doesn't lay directly on the skin.

Hemp leaves are just as useful, as the body does not absorb the THC from topical application.

Body potions

Warmed hemp oil rubbed gently into hair and covered with a plastic bag and left for about 1 hour (make sure no-one is coming round!) makes a great conditioner. Use once every two weeks.

The hemp oil can be rubbed onto dry skin. This is very effective, or it can be added to your favourite 100% natural essential oil and used in a relaxing bath. For a facial steam bath, place a few fresh sprigs of hemp along with other herbs such as rosemary, camomile and peppermint into a bowl and cover in boiling water. Cover your head with a towel and leaning over the bowl, breath deeply for about 5 minutes. Finally rinse your face in fresh warm water.

The squeezed juice from the leaves, rubbed into the scalp and left overnight, then combed out is said to keep nits away.

Further reading

The healing magic of cannabis

by Beverly Potter /Dan Joyt ISBN 1-57951-001-9.

A guide to marijuana in cool climates

by Don Irving ISBN 0-86166-126-5.

Nutritional and medicinal guide to hemp seed

by Kenneth Jones ISBN o-9625638-9-7.

Gold harvest

by George Mayfield ISBN 0-9530460- 0-1.

Marihuana the forbidden medicine

by Lester Grinspoon Md./James Bakalar ISBN 0-300-05994-9.

Marijuana myths marijuana facts

by Lynn Zimmer Ph.D./John P.Morgan, Md. ISBN 0-9641568-4-9.

Marijuana medical handbook

by Ed Rosenthal ISBN 0-932551-16-5.

Cannabis alchemy

by D. Gold ISBN 0-914171-40-2.

The emporer wears no clothes

by J. Herer ISBN 0-9524560-0-1.

Cooking with ganja

by Eric ISBN 0-9529299-0-2. Email: eric@peacefull-day.freeserve.co.uk

Weed World magazine (Vapourisation Pipe)

every 2 months ISSN 1362-3540. Web: www.users.dircon.co.uk/~weed1/

C.C.News

p.o.box 2700 Lewes, E.Sussex.uk (monthly) Email: bodaiju@solutions-inc.co.uk

The Bush Telegraph magazine

TBT. PO Box 176, Bicester D/O OX6 7RD Email: tbt@netmatters.co.uk

Campaign addresses

ACT (Alliance cannabis therapeutics)
P.O.BOX CR14, Leeds, LS7 4XF.

CLCIA (the campaign to legalize cannabis international association)
c/o 63 Peacock Street, Norwich, Norfolk NR3 1TB. Tel: 01603 625786
Email: webbooks@paston.co.uk

MMCO (medicinal marijuana Coop)
P.O.BOX 209,Stockport, England. SK5 8FB.

Transform
1 Rose Lake House, St George, Bristol B55 7HY.
Web: www.transformuk.freeserve.co.uk

Release
24-hr drug helpline Tel: 01717 299904

Outlets

Hemp paper: CHT, The malt house, Lyme Regis.Dorset

Hemp Union: 24,Anlaby Rd.Hull, HU1 2PA

Web: www.karoo.co.uk/hemp-union

Hemp Organics: 79 myddleton, Rd. Bounds Green, London

Power Seeds: P.o.box 3419 ferndown, BH22 9XR Tel/Fax: 01202 432212

Counter Culture (books): BCM Inspire, London WC1N 3XX

Eric's: P.o.box 2223 Dorchester, Dorset, DT1 2XH.

Web: www.peacefull-day.freeserve.co.uk/erics/

Freedom Books: 73 Fawcett rd, Southsea, Hants, PO4 0DB.

Web: www.freedombooks.co.uk

To order more copies write to:

P.O.BOX 2223, DORCHESTER, DORSET, DT1 2XH